Yakitori Cookbook 101

Master the Art of Japanese Grilled Skewers with Delicious Recipes and Techniques

YAKITORI COOKBOOK 101

First edition. November 6, 2023.

Written by john ahmad.

John Ahmad

Chapter Outline

Chapter 1: Introduction to Yakitori: A Brief History and Tradition

Welcome to the flavorful world of yakitori! In this chapter, we will delve into the origins, history, and cultural significance of this beloved Japanese culinary tradition. Gain a deeper understanding of the art of grilling skewered delights and the role yakitori plays in Japanese cuisine.

1.1 Origins of Yakitori:

Yakitori's origins can be traced back to the vibrant streets of Japan, where it emerged as a popular street food during the Edo period (1603-1868). Born out of necessity and ingenuity, yakitori offered a simple and affordable way to enjoy grilled chicken skewers. Initially, yakitori vendors used scraps of chicken meat, often the less desirable parts, to create these delectable skewers.

1.2 The Art of Yakitori:

Yakitori is more than just a method of cooking; it is a time-honored culinary art form that demands skill, precision, and respect for the ingredients. Learn about the traditional techniques and methods behind preparing and grilling yakitori. Discover the importance of choosing the right cuts of chicken, such as succulent thigh meat, tender breast, or flavorful wings, and how to properly marinate them to enhance their taste. Master the art of charcoal grilling, understanding the ideal heat, proper turning techniques, and the nuances of achieving the perfect char.

1.3 Yakitori Through the Ages:

Yakitori has undergone significant transformations throughout its history, adapting to societal changes and culinary innovations. From its humble beginnings as a street food, yakitori gradually gained popularity and found its place in izakayas (Japanese pubs), restaurants, and even gourmet establishments. Explore how yakitori evolved to incorporate a variety of meats, including pork, beef, and seafood, expanding the range of flavors and textures available to avid food enthusiasts.

1.4 Yakitori in Japanese Culture:

Yakitori is deeply ingrained in Japanese culture and reflects the country's values of simplicity, craftsmanship, and appreciation for nature's bounty. Discover how yakitori is not only a delicious meal but also a social experience. Learn about the communal aspect of yakitori dining, where friends, family, and colleagues gather around a grill, enjoying the aroma, conversation, and shared enjoyment of these grilled delicacies. Experience the vibrant atmosphere of yakitori bars, known as "yakitori-ya," where the clinking of skewers and lively conversations create a unique ambiance.

1.5 Regional Variations:

Japan's diverse regions offer a fascinating array of yakitori styles, each with its own distinct characteristics and flavors. Travel through the country and discover regional variations of yakitori, from Tokyo's Negima skewers featuring succulent chicken and scallions, to Hokkaido's grilled seafood skewers showcasing the bounty of the sea. Uncover the unique marinades, seasonings, and grilling techniques that have been passed down through generations, creating a rich tapestry of regional yakitori traditions.

As we conclude this chapter, you now have a comprehensive understanding of the origins, techniques, and cultural significance of yakitori. From its humble beginnings as a street food to its elevated status in Japanese cuisine, yakitori continues to captivate the hearts and taste buds of food lovers worldwide. With this foundation, you are ready to dive deeper into the world of yakitori, exploring an array of recipes, grilling tips, and creative variations that will elevate your culinary skills. Get ready to embark on a flavorful journey as we uncover the secrets of yakitori in the upcoming chapters.

Chapter 2: Essential Tools and Ingredients for Yakitori Preparation

To master the art of yakitori, it is important to have the right tools and ingredients at your disposal. In this chapter, we will explore the essential equipment, utensils, and ingredients needed to prepare delicious yakitori skewers. From traditional grilling apparatus to key flavor-enhancing components, this chapter will ensure you are well-equipped to create authentic and flavorful yakitori.

2.1 Grilling Equipment:

Grilling yakitori requires suitable equipment to achieve the desired flavors and textures. Traditionalists often opt for a shichirin, a small charcoal grill made of clay or ceramic. The shichirin provides intense heat and imparts a distinct smoky flavor to the skewers. Another popular option is a konro, a portable tabletop grill typically fueled by binchotan charcoal, known for its clean-burning and long-lasting properties. Alternatively, gas or electric grills can be used for convenience and precise temperature control. Regardless of the type of grill you choose, ensure it offers enough surface area for cooking multiple skewers simultaneously.

2.2 Skewers and Utensils:

Selecting the right skewers and utensils is essential for successful yakitori preparation. Bamboo skewers are a traditional choice, widely available and known for their ability to absorb moisture during grilling, imparting a subtle aroma to the skewers. They come in various lengths to accommodate different ingredients and can be soaked in water prior to use to prevent burning. Metal skewers, such as stainless steel or iron, offer durability and can be reused, making them a practical option for frequent yakitori cooking. Long-handled tongs are indispensable for turning and handling the skewers on the grill, while basting brushes are useful for glazing the skewers with marinades or sauces.

2.3 Ingredients for Yakitori:

The key to delicious yakitori lies in high-quality ingredients. Chicken is the most commonly used protein, with cuts like thigh meat, breast, wings, and even organ meats such as hearts and livers. Opt for free-range or organic chicken for superior flavor. When selecting other meats like pork, beef, or seafood, choose cuts that are suitable for grilling and have a good balance of lean meat and fat. Fresh vegetables like mushrooms, zucchini, bell peppers, and onions can also be used to create vegetarian or mixed skewers. It is important to source fresh, seasonal ingredients to ensure the best possible flavor.

2.4 Condiments and Accompaniments:

Enhance the flavors of your yakitori skewers with a variety of condiments and accompaniments. Tare, a sweet and savory soy-based glaze, is a traditional sauce used for yakitori. It can be made by combining soy sauce, mirin, sake, sugar, and other flavorings like ginger or garlic. Ponzu, a tangy citrus-based sauce, is another popular option for dipping yakitori. Experiment with different homemade or store-bought sauces to find your favorite flavor combinations. Accompany your yakitori with steamed rice, pickled vegetables, miso soup, or a fresh salad to complete the meal and create a balanced dining experience.

2.5 Essential Tips and Techniques:

To achieve delicious and perfectly cooked yakitori, there are several important tips and techniques to keep in mind. Properly marinating the ingredients is crucial for infusing them with flavor and ensuring tender results. Allow the meats to marinate for an adequate amount of time, typically a few hours or overnight, to maximize flavor absorption. Thread the ingredients onto the skewers evenly, leaving a small gap between each piece to ensure even cooking. When grilling, maintain a medium-high heat and avoid overcrowding the grill to prevent steaming and promote proper charring. Turn the skewers regularly to ensure they cook evenly and baste them with the marinade or glaze to add extra flavor and moisture. Keep a close eye on the skewers to prevent burning, adjusting the heat as needed.

Equipped with the knowledge of essential tools and ingredients for yakitori preparation, you are now ready to embark on your culinary journey. The right grilling equipment, skewers, utensils, and high-quality ingredients are the building blocks for creating authentic and flavorful yakitori. In the next chapter, we will explore the art of yakitori sauce variations, unlocking the secrets of traditional and creative twists that will elevate the taste of your skewers to new heights.

Chapter 3: Yakitori Sauce Variations: Traditional and Creative Twists

Yakitori sauce, also known as tare, is the flavorful essence that brings yakitori skewers to life. In this chapter, we will explore a range of yakitori sauce variations, from traditional recipes that pay homage to the authentic flavors of Japan to creative twists that infuse global influences. Whether you prefer the classic sweet and savory glaze or crave bold and innovative flavors, this chapter will inspire you to elevate your yakitori game.

3.1 Classic Yakitori Sauce:

The classic yakitori sauce is a balance of sweet and savory flavors, highlighting the umami notes of the grilled skewers. Here's a traditional recipe to get you started:

Ingredients:

- 1/2 cup soy sauce
- 1/4 cup mirin (sweet rice wine)
- 1/4 cup sake (Japanese rice wine)
- 2 tablespoons sugar

Instructions:

1. In a saucepan, combine soy sauce, mirin, sake, and sugar.
2. Heat the mixture over medium heat, stirring until the sugar dissolves.
3. Bring the sauce to a gentle boil, then reduce the heat to low and simmer for about 5 minutes until slightly thickened.
4. Remove from heat and let the sauce cool completely before using.

3.2 Teriyaki Glaze:

Teriyaki sauce adds a delightful glaze to yakitori skewers, infusing them with a rich, sweet, and tangy flavor profile. Here's a simple teriyaki glaze recipe:

Ingredients:

- 1/2 cup soy sauce
- 1/4 cup mirin
- 2 tablespoons sake
- 2 tablespoons sugar
- 1 tablespoon honey
- 1 clove garlic, minced
- 1 teaspoon grated ginger

Instructions:

1. In a saucepan, combine soy sauce, mirin, sake, sugar, honey, minced garlic, and grated ginger.
2. Stir the mixture well and bring it to a gentle boil over medium heat.
3. Reduce the heat to low and simmer for about 10 minutes, or until the sauce thickens to a glaze-like consistency.
4. Remove from heat and let the teriyaki glaze cool before using.

3.3 Spicy Miso Sauce:

For those who crave a bit of heat and depth, a spicy miso sauce is a delightful variation for your yakitori skewers. Here's a recipe to try:

Ingredients:

- 1/4 cup miso paste
- 2 tablespoons soy sauce
- 1 tablespoon sake
- 1 tablespoon mirin
- 1 tablespoon honey
- 1 teaspoon chili paste or Sriracha (adjust to taste)

- 1 clove garlic, minced
- 1 teaspoon grated ginger

Instructions:

1. In a bowl, whisk together miso paste, soy sauce, sake, mirin, honey, chili paste or Sriracha, minced garlic, and grated ginger until well combined.
2. Taste and adjust the spiciness level if desired by adding more chili paste or Sriracha.
3. Use the sauce immediately or let it sit for a while to allow the flavors to meld together.

3.4 Yakitori BBQ Sauce:

For a smoky and tangy twist on yakitori, try a homemade BBQ sauce that complements the grilled flavors perfectly. Here's a recipe to experiment with:

Ingredients:

- 1 cup ketchup
- 1/4 cup soy sauce
- 2 tablespoons mirin
- 2 tablespoons sake
- 2 tablespoons brown sugar
- 1 tablespoon Worcestershire sauce
- 1 tablespoon Dijon mustard
- 1 teaspoon garlic powder
- 1 teaspoon onion powder
- 1/2 teaspoon smoked paprika

Instructions:

1. In a saucepan, combine ketchup, soy sauce, mirin, sake, brown sugar, Worcestershire sauce, Dijon mustard, garlic powder, onion powder, and smoked paprika.
2. Whisk the ingredients together until well combined.
3. Heat the sauce over low heat, stirring occasionally, for about 10 minutes to allow the flavors to meld together.
4. Remove from heat and let the yakitori BBQ sauce cool before using.

Experiment with these classic and creative yakitori sauce variations to find your favorite flavor combinations. Remember, you can adjust the sweetness, tanginess, or spiciness according to your personal preference. In the next chapter, we will dive into classic chicken yakitori recipes, showcasing the traditional flavors and grilling techniques that make them irresistible.

Chapter 4: Classic Chicken Yakitori Recipes

Classic chicken yakitori is the epitome of grilled perfection, combining tender and juicy chicken with the irresistible flavors of yakitori sauce. In this chapter, we will explore a selection of traditional chicken yakitori recipes that will transport you to the streets of Japan. From succulent thigh meat to delectable chicken wings, these recipes will showcase the essence of authentic chicken yakitori.

4.1 Tsukune (Chicken Meatballs) Yakitori:

Tsukune is a beloved chicken yakitori variation featuring flavorful chicken meatballs. Here's a recipe to create these juicy and savory skewers:

Ingredients:

- 1 pound ground chicken
- 1/2 cup panko breadcrumbs
- 1/4 cup finely chopped green onions
- 2 tablespoons soy sauce
- 1 tablespoon mirin
- 1 tablespoon sake
- 1 tablespoon grated ginger
- 1 clove garlic, minced
- Salt and pepper to taste
- Bamboo skewers, soaked in water

Instructions:

1. In a bowl, combine ground chicken, panko breadcrumbs, green onions, soy sauce, mirin, sake, grated ginger, minced garlic, salt, and pepper. Mix well until all ingredients are evenly incorporated.

2. Divide the chicken mixture into small portions and shape them into oval meatballs.
3. Thread the meatballs onto soaked bamboo skewers, flattening them slightly to ensure even cooking.
4. Preheat your grill to medium-high heat and lightly oil the grates.
5. Grill the tsukune skewers for about 4-5 minutes per side, brushing them with yakitori sauce during the last few minutes of grilling.
6. Continue grilling until the chicken is fully cooked and has a delicious charred exterior.
7. Serve the tsukune yakitori skewers hot with additional yakitori sauce on the side.

4.2 Negima (Chicken and Scallion) Yakitori:

Negima yakitori combines succulent pieces of chicken with the vibrant flavors of grilled scallions. Follow this recipe to create these simple yet delightful skewers:

Ingredients:

- 1 pound boneless, skinless chicken thighs, cut into bite-sized pieces
- 4-5 scallions (green onions), cut into 2-inch lengths
- Yakitori sauce (refer to Chapter 3 for classic yakitori sauce recipe)
- Bamboo skewers, soaked in water

Instructions:

1. Thread the chicken pieces onto soaked bamboo skewers, alternating with scallion pieces. Leave a small gap between each ingredient for even cooking.
2. Preheat your grill to medium-high heat and lightly oil the grates.
3. Grill the negima skewers for about 4-5 minutes per side, brushing them with yakitori sauce during the last few minutes of grilling.
4. Continue grilling until the chicken is fully cooked and the scallions are lightly charred.
5. Remove from the grill and brush the skewers with additional yakitori sauce for extra flavor.
6. Serve the negima yakitori skewers hot with steamed rice and a side of yakitori sauce for dipping.

4.3 Momo (Chicken Thigh) Yakitori:

Momo yakitori showcases the juicy and flavorful chicken thighs, making it a classic and popular choice. Here's a recipe to create these mouthwatering skewers:

Ingredients:

- 1 pound boneless, skinless chicken thighs, cut into bite-sized pieces
- Yakitori sauce (refer to Chapter 3 for classic yakitori sauce recipe)
- Bamboo skewers, soaked in water

Instructions:

1. Thread the chicken thigh pieces onto soaked bamboo skewers, ensuring even spacing between each piece.
2. Preheat your grill to medium-high heat and lightly oil the grates.
3. Grill the momo skewers for about 4-5 minutes per side, brushing them with yakitori sauce during the last few minutes of grilling.
4. Continue grilling until the chicken is fully cooked and has a delightful charred exterior.
5. Remove from the grill and brush the skewers with additional yakitori sauce for extra flavor.
6. Serve the momo yakitori skewers hot with a side of steamed rice and yakitori sauce for dipping.

Enjoy the authentic flavors of these classic chicken yakitori recipes. The succulent meat, combined with the rich and savory yakitori sauce, will surely satisfy your cravings for this beloved Japanese dish. In the next chapter, we will explore the world of yakitori beyond chicken, venturing into pork, beef, and seafood skewers that will expand your culinary repertoire.

Chapter 5: Exploring Yakitori Beyond Chicken: Pork, Beef, and Seafood Skewers

While chicken is the star of classic yakitori, the world of yakitori expands far beyond poultry. In this chapter, we will venture into the realm of pork, beef, and seafood skewers, exploring the diverse and delicious options available. From succulent pork belly to savory beef skewers and delectable seafood morsels, these yakitori variations will broaden your culinary horizons and delight your taste buds.

1. Beef Sirloin Yakitori:

Beef sirloin yakitori offers a robust and savory twist to the traditional skewers. Try this recipe to experience the richness of beef in yakitori form:

Ingredients:

- 1 pound beef sirloin, cut into bite-sized cubes
- Yakitori sauce (refer to Chapter 3 for classic yakitori sauce recipe)
- Bamboo skewers, soaked in water

Instructions:

1. Thread the beef sirloin cubes onto soaked bamboo skewers, leaving a small gap between each piece.
2. Preheat your grill to medium-high heat and lightly oil the grates.
3. Grill the beef sirloin skewers for about 3-4 minutes per side, brushing them with yakitori sauce during the last minute of

grilling.

4. Continue grilling until the beef is cooked to your desired doneness, whether it's medium-rare, medium, or well-done.
5. Remove from the grill and brush the skewers with additional yakitori sauce for extra flavor.
6. Serve the beef sirloin yakitori skewers hot with a side of steamed rice and yakitori sauce for dipping.

5.3 Shrimp and Scallop Yakitori:

For seafood lovers, shrimp and scallop yakitori offers a delightful combination of flavors and textures. Follow this recipe to create these delectable skewers:

Ingredients:

- 1/2-pound large shrimp, peeled and deveined
- 1/2-pound scallops
- Yakitori sauce (refer to Chapter 3 for classic yakitori sauce recipe)
- Bamboo skewers, soaked in water.

Instructions:

1. Thread the shrimp and scallops onto soaked bamboo skewers, alternating between the two.
2. Preheat your grill to medium-high heat and lightly oil the grates.
3. Grill the shrimp and scallop skewers for about 2-3 minutes per side, brushing them with yakitori sauce during the last minute of grilling.
4. Continue grilling until the shrimp is pink and opaque and the scallops are cooked through.
5. Remove from the grill and brush the skewers with additional yakitori sauce for extra flavor.

6. Serve the shrimp and scallop yakitori skewers hot with a side of steamed rice and yakitori sauce for dipping.

Venture beyond chicken and explore the tantalizing world of pork, beef, and seafood yakitori. The succulent pork belly, savory beef sirloin, and delightful shrimp and scallop skewers will add variety and excitement to your yakitori repertoire. In the next chapter, we will delve into vegetarian and creative yakitori variations, showcasing the versatility and endless possibilities of this beloved Japanese dish.

Chapter 6: Vegetable Delights: Grilled Yakitori with a Twist of Greens

While yakitori is traditionally associated with meat and seafood, it's important to remember the versatility of this beloved Japanese dish. In this chapter, we will explore the world of vegetarian yakitori and creative twists that incorporate a variety of flavorful vegetables. From grilled mushrooms to vibrant skewers featuring colorful produce, these vegetable yakitori recipes will delight both vegetarians and those seeking a lighter, plant-based option.

6.1 Shiitake Mushroom Yakitori:

Shiitake mushrooms are a popular choice for vegetarian yakitori, offering a meaty texture and umami-rich flavor. Follow this recipe to create delicious shiitake mushroom yakitori skewers:

Ingredients:

- 1/2 pound shiitake mushrooms, stems removed
- Yakitori sauce (refer to Chapter 3 for classic yakitori sauce recipe)
- Bamboo skewers, soaked in water

Instructions:

1. Thread the shiitake mushrooms onto soaked bamboo skewers, cap side down.
2. Preheat your grill to medium-high heat and lightly oil the grates.
3. Grill the mushroom skewers for about 3-4 minutes per side, brushing them with yakitori sauce during the last minute of grilling.
4. Continue grilling until the mushrooms are tender and slightly charred.

5. Remove from the grill and brush the skewers with additional yakitori sauce for extra flavor.
6. Serve the shiitake mushroom yakitori skewers hot with a side of steamed rice and yakitori sauce for dipping.

6.2 Asparagus and Cherry Tomato Yakitori:

This vibrant yakitori variation combines the freshness of asparagus and the burst of sweetness from cherry tomatoes. Try this recipe for a delightful skewer of greens:

Ingredients:

- 1/2-pound asparagus, trimmed
- 1/2 cup cherry tomatoes
- Yakitori sauce (refer to Chapter 3 for classic yakitori sauce recipe)
- Bamboo skewers, soaked in water.

Instructions:

1. Thread the asparagus spears and cherry tomatoes onto soaked bamboo skewers, alternating between the two.
2. Preheat your grill to medium-high heat and lightly oil the grates.
3. Grill the skewers for about 2-3 minutes per side, brushing them with yakitori sauce during the last minute of grilling.
4. Continue grilling until the asparagus is crisp-tender and the cherry tomatoes are slightly charred.
5. Remove from the grill and brush the skewers with additional yakitori sauce for extra flavor.
6. Serve the asparagus and cherry tomato yakitori skewers hot with a side of steamed rice and yakitori sauce for dipping.

6.3 Bell Pepper and Onion Yakitori:

Colorful bell peppers and onions create a visually appealing and flavorful combination in this yakitori variation. Follow this recipe for a delightful skewer of vibrant vegetables:

Ingredients:

- 1 red bell pepper, cut into bite-sized pieces
- 1 green bell pepper, cut into bite-sized pieces
- 1 yellow bell pepper, cut into bite-sized pieces
- 1 red onion, cut into bite-sized pieces
- Yakitori sauce (refer to Chapter 3 for classic yakitori sauce recipe)
- Bamboo skewers, soaked in water

Instructions:

1. Thread the bell pepper and onion pieces onto soaked bamboo skewers, alternating between the colors.
2. Preheat your grill to medium-high heat and lightly oil the grates.
3. Grill the skewers for about 3-4 minutes per side, brushing them with yakitori sauce during the last minute of grilling.
4. Continue grilling until the vegetables are tender and lightly charred.
5. Remove from the grill and brush the skewers with additional yakitori sauce for extra flavor.
6. Serve the bell pepper and onion yakitori skewers hot with a side of steamed rice and yakitori sauce for dipping.

Embrace the delicious world of vegetarian yakitori by exploring these vegetable-centric variations. Whether you prefer the earthy flavor of shiitake mushrooms, the freshness of asparagus and cherry tomatoes, or the vibrant combination of bell peppers and onions, these vegetable yakitori recipes will satisfy your cravings for grilled goodness. In the next chapter, we will dive into creative twists and fusion-inspired yakitori recipes that will take your culinary adventure to new heights.

Chapter 7: Yakitori Fusion: Global Flavors Meet Traditional Japanese Grilling

Yakitori, with its simple yet flavorful profile, provides an excellent canvas for incorporating global flavors and culinary influences. In this chapter, we will explore the exciting world of yakitori fusion, where traditional Japanese grilling techniques merge with ingredients and seasonings from around the globe. From tangy teriyaki-glazed pineapple to spicy Thai-inspired chicken skewers, these fusion yakitori recipes will ignite your taste buds with a burst of international flavors.

7.1 Teriyaki-Glazed Pineapple Yakitori:

Take a tropical twist on traditional yakitori with this sweet and tangy pineapple skewer, glazed with a teriyaki sauce infused with island flavors.

Ingredients:

- 1 ripe pineapple, peeled and cut into bite-sized chunks
- Teriyaki glaze:
- 1/2 cup soy sauce
- 1/4 cup pineapple juice
- 2 tablespoons mirin
- 2 tablespoons brown sugar
- 1 tablespoon grated ginger
- 1 clove garlic, minced

Instructions:

1. Thread the pineapple chunks onto soaked bamboo skewers.
2. In a saucepan, combine soy sauce, pineapple juice, mirin, brown sugar, grated ginger, and minced garlic.
3. Heat the mixture over medium heat, stirring until the sugar

dissolves.

4. Bring the sauce to a gentle boil, then reduce the heat to low and simmer for about 5 minutes until slightly thickened.

5. Preheat your grill to medium-high heat and lightly oil the grates.

6. Grill the pineapple skewers for about 2-3 minutes per side, brushing them with the teriyaki glaze during the last minute of grilling.

7. Continue grilling until the pineapple is caramelized and has a slight char.

8. Remove from the grill and brush the skewers with additional teriyaki glaze for extra flavor.

9. Serve the teriyaki-glazed pineapple yakitori skewers hot as a sweet and tangy appetizer or dessert.

7.2 Thai-inspired Chicken Satay Yakitori:

Infuse your yakitori with the vibrant flavors of Thai cuisine with this chicken satay-inspired skewer, featuring a peanut-based marinade and a zesty dipping sauce.

Ingredients:

- 1 pound boneless, skinless chicken thighs, cut into thin strips
- Marinade:
- 1/4 cup soy sauce
- 2 tablespoons coconut milk
- 1 tablespoon fish sauce
- 1 tablespoon lime juice
- 1 tablespoon brown sugar
- 1 teaspoon curry powder
- 1 clove garlic, minced
- 1 teaspoon grated ginger
- Peanut Dipping Sauce:
- 1/4 cup creamy peanut butter

- 2 tablespoons soy sauce
- 1 tablespoon lime juice
- 1 tablespoon honey
- 1 teaspoon fish sauce
- 1/2 teaspoon Sriracha (optional)
- Water (as needed to achieve desired consistency)

Instructions:

1. In a bowl, whisk together soy sauce, coconut milk, fish sauce, lime juice, brown sugar, curry powder, minced garlic, and grated ginger to make the marinade.
2. Add the chicken strips to the marinade and toss to coat. Cover and refrigerate for at least 1 hour, allowing the flavors to meld.
3. Preheat your grill to medium-high heat and lightly oil the grates.
4. Thread the marinated chicken strips onto soaked bamboo skewers, shaking off any excess marinade.
5. Grill the chicken satay skewers for about 3-4 minutes per side, or until cooked through with a slight char.
6. Meanwhile, prepare the peanut dipping sauce by combining peanut butter, soy sauce, lime juice, honey, fish sauce, and Sriracha (if using) in a bowl. Add water gradually, stirring, until the desired dipping consistency is achieved.
7. Serve the Thai-inspired chicken satay yakitori skewers hot with the peanut dipping sauce on the side.

7.3 Mediterranean-inspired Lamb and Vegetable Yakitori:

Infuse your yakitori with Mediterranean flavors by combining succulent lamb and vibrant vegetables with a zesty marinade featuring herbs and citrus.

Ingredients:

- 1 pound lamb leg or shoulder, cut into bite-sized cubes
- Assorted vegetables of your choice, such as cherry tomatoes, zucchini, and bell peppers, cut into bite-sized pieces

Marinade:

- 1/4 cup olive oil
- 2 tablespoons lemon juice
- 2 cloves garlic, minced
- 1 teaspoon dried oregano
- 1 teaspoon dried thyme
- 1/2 teaspoon paprika
- Salt and pepper to taste

Instructions:

1. In a bowl, whisk together olive oil, lemon juice, minced garlic, dried oregano, dried thyme, paprika, salt, and pepper to make the marinade.
2. Add the lamb cubes to the marinade and toss to coat. Cover and refrigerate for at least 1 hour to allow the flavors to meld.
3. Preheat your grill to medium-high heat and lightly oil the grates.
4. Thread the marinated lamb cubes and vegetable pieces onto soaked bamboo skewers, alternating between them.
5. Grill the lamb and vegetable skewers for about 3-4 minutes per side, or until the lamb is cooked to your desired doneness and the vegetables are tender-crisp.
6. Remove from the grill and let the skewers rest for a few minutes before serving.
7. Serve the Mediterranean-inspired lamb and vegetable yakitori skewers hot with a side of couscous or a fresh salad.

Unleash your creativity with fusion-inspired yakitori recipes, where global flavors merge harmoniously with traditional Japanese grilling. Whether it's the tropical tang of teriyaki-glazed pineapple, the zesty Thai-inspired chicken satay, or the Mediterranean-infused lamb and vegetable skewers, these fusion yakitori recipes will transport your taste buds on an exciting culinary adventure. In the next chapter, we will explore tantalizing side dishes and accompaniments that perfectly complement the flavors of yakitori.

Chapter 8: Yakitori Party Platters: Entertaining with Skewers

Yakitori is not only a delicious and versatile dish but also a fantastic option for entertaining guests. In this chapter, we will delve into the world of yakitori party platters, providing you with ideas and inspiration for creating beautiful and flavorful spreads that will impress your friends and family. From themed platters to customizable options, these yakitori party platters will elevate your gatherings to a whole new level of culinary delight.

8.1 Traditional Yakitori Feast:

Celebrate the essence of traditional yakitori with a platter that features an assortment of classic skewers. Here's a sample arrangement:

Chicken Momo (Thigh) Yakitori:

Ingredients:

- 1 pound boneless, skinless chicken thighs, cut into bite-sized pieces
- Yakitori sauce (refer to Chapter 3 for classic yakitori sauce recipe)
- Bamboo skewers, soaked in water

Instructions:

1. Thread the chicken thigh pieces onto soaked bamboo skewers, ensuring even spacing between each piece.
2. Preheat your grill to medium-high heat and lightly oil the grates.
3. Grill the momo skewers for about 4-5 minutes per side,

brushing them with yakitori sauce during the last few minutes of grilling.

4. Continue grilling until the chicken is fully cooked and has a delightful charred exterior.
5. Remove from the grill and brush the skewers with additional yakitori sauce for extra flavor.
6. Serve the momo yakitori skewers hot with a side of steamed rice and yakitori sauce for dipping.

Chicken Negima (Chicken and Scallion) Yakitori:
Ingredients:

- 1-pound boneless, skinless chicken thighs, cut into bite-sized pieces
- 4-5 scallions (green onions), cut into 2-inch lengths
- Yakitori sauce (refer to Chapter 3 for classic yakitori sauce recipe)
- Bamboo skewers, soaked in water

Instructions:

1. Thread the chicken pieces onto soaked bamboo skewers, alternating with scallion pieces. Leave a small gap between each ingredient for even cooking.
2. Preheat your grill to medium-high heat and lightly oil the grates.
3. Grill the negima skewers for about 4-5 minutes per side, brushing them with yakitori sauce during the last few minutes of grilling.
4. Continue grilling until the chicken is fully cooked and the scallions are lightly charred.
5. Remove from the grill and brush the skewers with additional yakitori sauce for extra flavor.

6. Serve the negima yakitori skewers hot with steamed rice and a side of yakitori sauce for dipping.

Tsukune (Chicken Meatballs) Yakitori:
Ingredients:

- 1 pound ground chicken
- 1/2 cup panko breadcrumbs
- 1/4 cup finely chopped green onions
- 2 tablespoons soy sauce
- 1 tablespoon mirin
- 1 tablespoon sake
- 1 tablespoon grated ginger
- 1 clove garlic, minced
- Salt and pepper to taste
- Bamboo skewers, soaked in water

Instructions:

1. In a bowl, combine ground chicken, panko breadcrumbs, green onions, soy sauce, mirin, sake, grated ginger, minced garlic, salt, and pepper. Mix well until all ingredients are evenly incorporated.
2. Divide the chicken mixture into small portions and shape them into oval meatballs.
3. Thread the meatballs onto soaked bamboo skewers, flattening them slightly to ensure even cooking.
4. Preheat your grill to medium-high heat and lightly oil the grates.
5. Grill the tsukune skewers for about 4-5 minutes per side, brushing them with yakitori sauce during the last few minutes of grilling.
6. Continue grilling until the chicken is fully cooked and has a delicious charred exterior.
7. Serve the tsukune yakitori skewers hot with additional yakitori sauce on the side..

Shiitake Mushroom Yakitori:

Ingredients:

- 1/2 pound shiitake mushrooms, stems removed
- Yakitori sauce (refer to Chapter 3 for classic yakitori sauce recipe)
- Bamboo skewers, soaked in water

Instructions:

1. Thread the shiitake mushrooms onto soaked bamboo skewers, cap side down.
2. Preheat your grill to medium-high heat and lightly oil the grates.
3. Grill the mushroom skewers for about 3-4 minutes per side, brushing them with yakitori sauce during the last minute of grilling.
4. Continue grilling until the mushrooms are tender and slightly charred.
5. Remove from the grill and brush the skewers with additional yakitori sauce for extra flavor.
6. Serve the shiitake mushroom yakitori skewers hot with a side of steamed rice and yakitori sauce for dipping.

Arrange the skewers on a large platter, creating an appealing display of various textures and flavors. Serve with steamed rice, a bowl of yakitori sauce for dipping, and traditional sides such as pickled vegetables, miso soup, and Japanese-style potato salad.

8.2 Surf and Turf Fusion:

Combine the best of land and sea with a surf and turf-themed yakitori platter. Here's a sample arrangement:

Beef Sirloin Yakitori:

Ingredients:

- 1 pound beef sirloin, cut into bite-sized cubes
- Yakitori sauce (refer to Chapter 3 for classic yakitori sauce recipe)
- Bamboo skewers, soaked in water

Instructions:

1. Thread the beef sirloin cubes onto soaked bamboo skewers, leaving a small gap between each piece.
2. Preheat your grill to medium-high heat and lightly oil the grates.
3. Grill the beef sirloin skewers for about 3-4 minutes per side, brushing them with yakitori sauce during the last minute of grilling.
4. Continue grilling until the beef is cooked to your desired doneness, whether it's medium-rare, medium, or well-done.
5. Remove from the grill and brush the skewers with additional yakitori sauce for extra flavor.
6. Serve the beef sirloin yakitori skewers hot with a side of steamed rice and yakitori sauce for dipping.

Shrimp and Scallop Yakitori:

Ingredients:

- 1/2 pound large shrimp, peeled and deveined
- 1/2 pound scallops

- Yakitori sauce (refer to Chapter 3 for classic yakitori sauce recipe)
- Bamboo skewers, soaked in water

Instructions:

1. Thread the shrimp and scallops onto soaked bamboo skewers, alternating between the two.
2. Preheat your grill to medium-high heat and lightly oil the grates.
3. Grill the shrimp and scallop skewers for about 2-3 minutes per side, brushing them with yakitori sauce during the last minute of grilling.
4. Continue grilling until the shrimp is pink and opaque and the scallops are cooked through.
5. Remove from the grill and brush the skewers with additional yakitori sauce for extra flavor.
6. Serve the shrimp and scallop yakitori skewers hot with a side of steamed rice and yakitori sauce for dipping.

Bell Pepper and Onion Yakitori:
Ingredients:

- 1 red bell pepper, cut into bite-sized pieces
- 1 green bell pepper, cut into bite-sized pieces
- 1 yellow bell pepper, cut into bite-sized pieces
- 1 red onion, cut into bite-sized pieces
- Yakitori sauce (refer to Chapter 3 for classic yakitori sauce recipe)
- Bamboo skewers, soaked in water

Instructions:

1. Thread the bell pepper and onion pieces onto soaked bamboo skewers, alternating between the colors.
2. Preheat your grill to medium-high heat and lightly oil the grates.
3. Grill the skewers for about 3-4 minutes per side, brushing them with yakitori sauce during the last minute of grilling.
4. Continue grilling until the vegetables are tender and lightly charred.
5. Remove from the grill and brush the skewers with additional yakitori sauce for extra flavor.
6. Serve the bell pepper and onion yakitori skewers hot with a side of steamed rice and yakitori sauce for dipping.

Arrange the skewers on a platter, alternating between the beef, seafood, and vegetable options. Serve with a side of teriyaki glaze for dipping, along with a refreshing cucumber and seaweed salad, roasted potatoes, and crusty bread.

8.3 Vegetarian Delight:

Cater to vegetarian guests with a vibrant and flavorful vegetarian yakitori platter. Here's a sample arrangement:

Grilled Tofu Yakitori:

Ingredients:

- 1 block of firm tofu, cut into bite-sized cubes
- Yakitori sauce (refer to Chapter 3 for classic yakitori sauce recipe)
- Bamboo skewers, soaked in water

Instructions:

1. Thread the tofu cubes onto soaked bamboo skewers, leaving a small gap between each piece.
2. Preheat your grill to medium-high heat and lightly oil the grates.
3. Grill the tofu skewers for about 3-4 minutes per side, brushing them with yakitori sauce during the last minute of grilling.
4. Continue grilling until the tofu is nicely charred and heated through.
5. Remove from the grill and brush the skewers with additional yakitori sauce for extra flavor.
6. Serve the grilled tofu yakitori skewers hot with a side of steamed rice and yakitori sauce for dipping.

Asparagus and Cherry Tomato Yakitori:

Ingredients:

- 1/2 pound asparagus spears, trimmed
- 1/2 cup cherry tomatoes
- Yakitori sauce (refer to Chapter 3 for classic yakitori sauce recipe)

- Bamboo skewers, soaked in water

Instructions:

1. Thread the asparagus spears and cherry tomatoes onto soaked bamboo skewers, alternating between the two.
2. Preheat your grill to medium-high heat and lightly oil the grates.
3. Grill the skewers for about 2-3 minutes per side, brushing them with yakitori sauce during the last minute of grilling.
4. Continue grilling until the asparagus is crisp-tender and the cherry tomatoes are slightly charred.
5. Remove from the grill and brush the skewers with additional yakitori sauce for extra flavor.
6. Serve the asparagus and cherry tomato yakitori skewers hot with a side of steamed rice and yakitori sauce for dipping.

Shiitake Mushroom Yakitori:
Ingredients:

- 1/2 pound shiitake mushrooms, stems removed
- Yakitori sauce (refer to Chapter 3 for classic yakitori sauce recipe)
- Bamboo skewers, soaked in water

Instructions:

1. Thread the shiitake mushrooms onto soaked bamboo skewers, cap side down.
2. Preheat your grill to medium-high heat and lightly oil the grates.
3. Grill the mushroom skewers for about 3-4 minutes per side, brushing them with yakitori sauce during the last minute of grilling.
4. Continue grilling until the mushrooms are tender and slightly charred.
5. Remove from the grill and brush the skewers with additional yakitori sauce for extra flavor.
6. Serve the shiitake mushroom yakitori skewers hot with a side of steamed rice and yakitori sauce for dipping.

Bell Pepper and Onion Yakitori:
Ingredients:

- 1 red bell pepper, cut into bite-sized pieces
- 1 green bell pepper, cut into bite-sized pieces
- 1 yellow bell pepper, cut into bite-sized pieces
- 1 red onion, cut into bite-sized pieces
- Yakitori sauce (refer to Chapter 3 for classic yakitori sauce recipe)
- Bamboo skewers, soaked in water

Instructions:

1. Thread the bell pepper and onion pieces onto soaked bamboo skewers, alternating between the colors.
2. Preheat your grill to medium-high heat and lightly oil the grates.
3. Grill the skewers for about 3-4 minutes per side, brushing them with yakitori sauce during the last minute of grilling.
4. Continue grilling until the vegetables are tender and lightly charred.
5. Remove from the grill and brush the skewers with additional yakitori sauce for extra flavor.
6. Serve the bell pepper and onion yakitori skewers hot with a side of steamed rice and yakitori sauce for dipping.

Arrange the skewers on a platter, creating a colorful display of vegetarian delights. Serve with a side of ponzu sauce for dipping, along with steamed jasmine rice, a mixed green salad, and a variety of pickled vegetables.

8.4 Build-Your-Own Yakitori Bar:

Engage your guests by setting up a build-your-own yakitori bar, allowing them to customize their skewers with a variety of ingredients and toppings. Here's what you can include:

Assorted proteins: Chicken, pork, beef, seafood, and tofu

Assorted vegetables: Bell peppers, onions, zucchini, mushrooms, cherry tomatoes, asparagus

Assorted sauces: Classic yakitori sauce, teriyaki glaze, peanut sauce, spicy miso sauce

Toppings and garnishes: Chopped scallions, sesame seeds, cilantro, grated ginger, shredded nori

Provide guests with skewers and let them create their own combinations. Set up a grill station where they can cook their skewers to perfection. Offer a variety of side dishes like steamed rice, edamame, and a fresh fruit platter to complete the experience.

With these yakitori party platter ideas, you can impress your guests with visually stunning displays and a variety of flavors to suit different tastes. Whether you opt for a traditional feast, a surf and turf fusion, a vegetarian delight, or a build-your-own bar, these platters will make your yakitori gatherings a memorable and enjoyable experience. In the next chapter, we will explore creative twists on yakitori-inspired desserts and sweet treats.

Chapter 9: Mastering Yakitori Techniques: Tips for Perfect Grilling

Grilling yakitori requires skill and precision to achieve the perfect balance of flavors and textures. In this chapter, we will share valuable tips and techniques that will elevate your yakitori grilling game. From preparing the skewers to controlling the grill temperature, these expert tips will help you become a master of yakitori and ensure each bite is a succulent delight.

9.1 Choosing the Right Skewers:

Bamboo Skewers: Soak bamboo skewers in water for at least 30 minutes before grilling to prevent them from burning on the grill. This also helps to keep the ingredients moist and prevents them from sticking to the skewers.

Metal Skewers: If you prefer reusable and heat-resistant options, invest in stainless steel or metal skewers. These provide even heat distribution and are less likely to burn or break.

9.2 Preparing Ingredients:

Uniform Sizing: Cut the ingredients into uniform sizes to ensure even cooking. This helps to prevent some pieces from being overcooked while others remain undercooked.

Marinating: Marinate the ingredients for at least 30 minutes or up to overnight to enhance flavor. Ensure the marinade is well-distributed, allowing each piece to absorb the delicious flavors.

9.3 Controlling Grill Temperature:

High Heat: Preheat your grill to medium-high heat (around 400°F to 450°F) for the initial searing and charring of the ingredients. This helps to lock in the juices and create that delightful smoky flavor.

Medium Heat: After searing, reduce the heat to medium (around 350°F to 375°F) for a slower and more controlled cooking process. This allows the ingredients to cook through without burning the outer layers.

9.4 Basting with Sauce:

Basting: Brush the yakitori sauce or marinade onto the skewers during the last few minutes of grilling. This adds an extra layer of flavor and creates a caramelized glaze.

Multiple Layers: Apply the sauce in multiple layers, allowing each layer to caramelize before adding the next. This builds up a rich and savory coating on the skewers.

9.5 Timing and Doneness:

Timing: Keep a close eye on the grilling time to ensure the ingredients are cooked to perfection. Overcooking can lead to dry and tough skewers, while undercooking may result in unsafe consumption.

Doneness: Use a meat thermometer to check the internal temperature of meats such as chicken and pork. Chicken should reach an internal temperature of 165°F, while pork should reach 145°F.

9.6 Resting and Serving:

Resting: Allow the cooked skewers to rest for a few minutes before serving. This helps the juices distribute evenly, resulting in more succulent and flavorful bites.

Serving: Arrange the yakitori skewers on a platter and serve them immediately while they are still hot. Pair them with complementary sauces, dips, and sides for a complete yakitori experience.

By following these yakitori grilling techniques, you'll be able to achieve perfectly cooked skewers every time. Remember to pay attention to the skewer choice, prepare the ingredients with care, control the grill temperature, baste with sauce for flavor, time the grilling process accurately, and let the skewers rest before serving.

Chapter 10: Yakitori Dips and Accompaniments: Elevating the Flavor Experience

Yakitori skewers are delicious on their own, but pairing them with the right dips and accompaniments can take the flavor experience to a whole new level. In this chapter, we will explore a variety of dips, sauces, and side dishes that complement the savory goodness of yakitori. From traditional classics to creative twists, these accompaniments will enhance your yakitori feast and leave your taste buds craving for more.

10.1 Classic Yakitori Sauce:

Ingredients:

- 1/2 cup soy sauce
- 1/4 cup mirin
- 1/4 cup sake
- 2 tablespoons sugar

Instructions:

1. In a saucepan, combine the soy sauce, mirin, sake, and sugar.
2. Place the saucepan over medium heat and stir until the sugar has dissolved.
3. Simmer the sauce for about 5 minutes, allowing the flavors to meld together.
4. Remove from heat and let the sauce cool before using.
5. Serve the classic yakitori sauce in small dipping bowls alongside the yakitori skewers.

10.2 Ponzu Sauce:

Ingredients:

- 1/4 cup soy sauce

- 2 tablespoons fresh lemon juice
- 1 tablespoon rice vinegar
- 1 tablespoon mirin
- 1 tablespoon bonito flakes (optional)
- 1 teaspoon grated ginger
- 1 teaspoon grated daikon radish

Instructions:

1. In a bowl, combine the soy sauce, lemon juice, rice vinegar, mirin, bonito flakes (if using), grated ginger, and grated daikon radish.
2. Stir well to blend the ingredients together.
3. Let the ponzu sauce sit for about 15 minutes to allow the flavors to develop.
4. Strain the sauce to remove any solids, if desired.
5. Serve the ponzu sauce in small dipping bowls alongside the yakitori skewers.

10.3 Spicy Miso Sauce:
Ingredients:

- 1/4 cup white miso paste
- 2 tablespoons soy sauce
- 2 tablespoons mirin
- 1 tablespoon sesame oil
- 1 tablespoon sriracha or chili paste
- 1 tablespoon sugar
- 1 teaspoon grated garlic

Instructions:

1. In a bowl, whisk together the white miso paste, soy sauce, mirin, sesame oil, sriracha or chili paste, sugar, and grated garlic.
2. Continue whisking until the sauce is smooth and well combined.
3. Taste and adjust the spiciness or sweetness to your liking.
4. Serve the spicy miso sauce in small dipping bowls alongside the yakitori skewers.

10.4 Side Dishes and Accompaniments:

Steamed Rice: Serve fluffy steamed rice as a staple side dish to complement the flavors of yakitori.

Miso Soup: Prepare a comforting bowl of miso soup with tofu, seaweed, and scallions to add warmth and depth to the meal.

Japanese Potato Salad: Enjoy the creamy and tangy flavors of Japanese-style potato salad, made with potatoes, carrots, cucumber, mayonnaise, and a touch of vinegar.

Pickled Vegetables: Add a refreshing and tangy element to the meal with a variety of pickled vegetables such as cucumbers, radishes, and cabbage.

Edamame: Serve a bowl of steamed edamame, lightly salted, as a nutritious and addictive snack.

Green Salad: Balance the meal with a simple green salad dressed with a light vinaigrette or sesame dressing.

Tsukemono: Explore the world of Japanese pickles known as tsukemono, which can range from crunchy cucumber pickles to tangy daikon radish pickles.

10.5 Beverage Pairings:

Sake: Enhance the flavors of yakitori with a glass of chilled sake, such as Junmai or Ginjo, which complements the smoky and savory notes.

Japanese Whisky: Sip on a smooth and rich Japanese whisky to accompany the grilled flavors of yakitori.

Green Tea: Enjoy a cup of traditional Japanese green tea, either hot or iced, for a refreshing and cleansing beverage option.

Experiment with different combinations of dips, sauces, and side dishes to find your favorite flavor pairings with yakitori. Whether you prefer the classic yakitori sauce, the tangy ponzu sauce, or the spicy miso sauce, these dips will add depth and complexity to your yakitori feast. And don't forget to explore the variety of side dishes and beverage pairings to create a well-rounded and memorable dining experience.

Chapter 11: Yakitori for Special Diets: Gluten-Free, Vegetarian, and Vegan Options

Yakitori is a versatile dish that can be adapted to accommodate different dietary needs. In this chapter, we will explore gluten-free, vegetarian, and vegan options for enjoying the flavors of yakitori. Whether you have dietary restrictions or are looking to offer a variety of options to cater to different preferences, these recipes will ensure that everyone can indulge in the deliciousness of yakitori.

11.1 Gluten-Free Yakitori:

For those following a gluten-free diet, it's important to be mindful of the sauces and ingredients used in yakitori. Here are some gluten-free options to enjoy:

Gluten-Free Yakitori Sauce:

Ingredients:

- 1/2 cup gluten-free soy sauce
- 1/4 cup mirin (ensure it's gluten-free)
- 1/4 cup sake (ensure it's gluten-free)
- 2 tablespoons sugar

Instructions:

1. In a saucepan, combine the gluten-free soy sauce, mirin, sake, and sugar.
2. Place the saucepan over medium heat and stir until the sugar has dissolved.
3. Simmer the sauce for about 5 minutes, allowing the flavors to meld together.

4. Remove from heat and let the sauce cool before using.

5. Serve the gluten-free yakitori sauce in small dipping bowls alongside the yakitori skewers.

Note: When selecting other ingredients for your yakitori, make sure they are gluten-free. Opt for gluten-free tamari instead of soy sauce and check the labels of other condiments to ensure they are free from gluten.

11.2 Vegetarian Yakitori:

For vegetarian yakitori, we will replace meat with plant-based alternatives and focus on showcasing the flavors of vegetables. Here are some vegetarian options to try:

Grilled Tofu Yakitori:

Ingredients:

- 1 block of firm tofu, cut into bite-sized cubes
- Vegetarian yakitori sauce (refer to Chapter 3 for classic yakitori sauce recipe or use a vegetarian alternative)
- Bamboo skewers, soaked in water

Instructions:

1. Thread the tofu cubes onto soaked bamboo skewers, leaving a small gap between each piece.
2. Preheat your grill to medium-high heat and lightly oil the grates.
3. Grill the tofu skewers for about 3-4 minutes per side, brushing them with vegetarian yakitori sauce during the last minute of grilling.
4. Continue grilling until the tofu is nicely charred and heated through.
5. Remove from the grill and brush the skewers with additional vegetarian yakitori sauce for extra flavor.
6. Serve the grilled tofu yakitori skewers hot with a side of steamed rice and vegetarian yakitori sauce for dipping.

Asparagus and Mushroom Yakitori:

Ingredients:

- 1/2 pound asparagus spears, trimmed
- 1/2 pound shiitake mushrooms, stems removed
- Vegetarian yakitori sauce (refer to Chapter 3 for classic yakitori

sauce recipe or use a vegetarian alternative)
- Bamboo skewers, soaked in water

Instructions:

1. Thread the asparagus spears and shiitake mushrooms onto soaked bamboo skewers, alternating between the two.
2. Preheat your grill to medium-high heat and lightly oil the grates.
3. Grill the skewers for about 3-4 minutes per side, brushing them with vegetarian yakitori sauce during the last minute of grilling.
4. Continue grilling until the asparagus is crisp-tender and the mushrooms are tender and slightly charred.
5. Remove from the grill and brush the skewers with additional vegetarian yakitori sauce for extra flavor.
6. Serve the asparagus and mushroom yakitori skewers hot with a side of steamed rice and vegetarian yakitori sauce for dipping.

Explore a variety of vegetables such as bell peppers, zucchini, cherry tomatoes, and eggplant to create your own vegetarian yakitori combinations. Pair them with a range of vegetarian sauces and dips for a flavorful and satisfying experience.

11.3 Vegan Yakitori:

For a vegan twist on yakitori, we will use plant-based protein sources and flavor-packed marinades. Here are some vegan options to enjoy:

Grilled Seitan Yakitori:

Ingredients:

- 1 pound seitan, cut into bite-sized pieces
- Vegan yakitori sauce (refer to Chapter 3 for classic yakitori sauce recipe or use a vegan alternative)

- Bamboo skewers, soaked in water

Instructions:

1. Thread the seitan pieces onto soaked bamboo skewers, leaving a small gap between each piece.
2. Preheat your grill to medium-high heat and lightly oil the grates.
3. Grill the seitan skewers for about 3-4 minutes per side, brushing them with vegan yakitori sauce during the last minute of grilling.
4. Continue grilling until the seitan is nicely charred and heated through.
5. Remove from the grill and brush the skewers with additional vegan yakitori sauce for extra flavor.
6. Serve the grilled seitan yakitori skewers hot with a side of steamed rice and vegan yakitori sauce for dipping.

Grilled Portobello Mushroom Yakitori:
Ingredients:

- 4 large portobello mushroom caps
- Vegan yakitori sauce (refer to Chapter 3 for classic yakitori sauce recipe or use a vegan alternative)
- Bamboo skewers, soaked in water

Instructions:

1. Remove the stems from the portobello mushroom caps and gently scrape out the gills.
2. Thread the mushroom caps onto soaked bamboo skewers, cap side down.

3. Preheat your grill to medium-high heat and lightly oil the grates.
4. Grill the mushroom skewers for about 4-5 minutes per side, brushing them with vegan yakitori sauce during the last minute of grilling.
5. Continue grilling until the mushrooms are tender and lightly charred.
6. Remove from the grill and brush the skewers with additional vegan yakitori sauce for extra flavor.
7. Serve the grilled portobello mushroom yakitori skewers hot with a side of steamed rice and vegan yakitori sauce for dipping.

Experiment with other vegan protein sources like tempeh or tofu and a variety of vegetables to create your own vegan yakitori combinations. Pair them with vegan-friendly sauces and dips for a delectable plant-based yakitori experience.

Remember to always check the labels of your ingredients and condiments to ensure they meet your specific dietary requirements. With these gluten-free, vegetarian, and vegan yakitori options, you can enjoy the flavors of yakitori while catering to special diets.

Chapter 12: Grilling with Charcoal vs. Gas: Pros and Cons

When it comes to grilling yakitori, one of the decisions you'll face is whether to use charcoal or gas as your heat source. Each method has its own set of pros and cons that can affect the flavor, convenience, and overall grilling experience. In this chapter, we'll compare grilling with charcoal and gas, highlighting their advantages and disadvantages, so you can make an informed choice that suits your preferences and circumstances.

12.1 Grilling with Charcoal:

Grilling with charcoal has long been cherished for its smoky flavor and traditional appeal. Here are the pros and cons of using charcoal for yakitori:

Pros:

Smoky Flavor: Charcoal grilling infuses a distinct smoky flavor into the yakitori, adding depth and richness to the taste.

High Heat: Charcoal grills can reach higher temperatures than gas grills, allowing for better searing and charring of the yakitori.

Authentic Experience: Many grill enthusiasts appreciate the ritual and authenticity of cooking over charcoal, as it connects them to grilling traditions.

Cons:

Longer Preheat Time: Charcoal grills require more time to preheat and reach the desired cooking temperature, which can delay the grilling process.

More Complex Setup: Setting up a charcoal grill involves arranging the charcoal, lighting it, and waiting for it to reach the optimal cooking temperature. It requires some skill and practice to achieve consistent results.

Cleanup and Maintenance: Ashes need to be properly disposed of, and cleaning the grill can be more involved due to the accumulation of charcoal residue.

12.2 Grilling with Gas:

Gas grills offer convenience and control, making them a popular choice for outdoor cooking. Let's explore the pros and cons of grilling with gas for yakitori:

Pros:

Ease of Use: Gas grills are quick to start, reaching the desired cooking temperature within minutes. They offer precise temperature control, allowing for more consistent results.

Convenience: Gas grills eliminate the need to handle and manage charcoal, making them easier to operate, especially for beginners or those short on time.

Lower Cleanup Effort: Gas grills produce minimal ash and residue, simplifying the cleanup process. Additionally, some gas grills come with removable grease trays that collect drippings for easy disposal.

Cons:

Less Smoky Flavor: Gas grills lack the distinct smoky flavor that charcoal imparts, which may result in slightly different taste profiles for the yakitori.

Lower Maximum Heat: Gas grills generally have a lower maximum heat compared to charcoal grills, which can affect the searing and charring capabilities.

Limited Portability: Gas grills typically require a steady fuel source, such as propane tanks or a natural gas connection, making them less portable than charcoal grills.

Ultimately, the choice between charcoal and gas grilling comes down to personal preference, convenience, and the flavor profile you desire for your yakitori. If you prioritize the smoky flavor and are willing to invest time in preheating and maintaining a charcoal grill, it can be a rewarding experience. On the other hand, if ease of use, quick start-up, and precise temperature control are important to you, a gas grill might be a better fit.

Consider your lifestyle, cooking preferences, and available space when deciding which grilling method to use for your yakitori adventures. Whichever option you choose, the joy of grilling and savoring delicious yakitori will be a delightful experience.

Chapter 13: Yakitori Sides and Salads: Complementing the Skewered Delights

While yakitori skewers take center stage, a well-rounded meal is incomplete without delicious side dishes and refreshing salads. In this chapter, we will explore a variety of yakitori-inspired sides and salads that perfectly complement the flavors of the grilled skewers. From vibrant vegetable dishes to light and tangy salads, these accompaniments will elevate your yakitori feast to new heights.

13.1 Cucumber and Seaweed Salad:

Ingredients:

- 2 cucumbers, thinly sliced
- 1 cup wakame seaweed, rehydrated
- 2 tablespoons rice vinegar
- 1 tablespoon soy sauce
- 1 tablespoon sesame oil
- 1 teaspoon sugar
- Sesame seeds, for garnish

Instructions:

1. In a bowl, combine the sliced cucumbers and rehydrated wakame seaweed.
2. In a separate small bowl, whisk together the rice vinegar, soy sauce, sesame oil, and sugar to make the dressing.
3. Pour the dressing over the cucumber and seaweed mixture. Toss gently to coat.
4. Let the salad marinate in the refrigerator for at least 30 minutes to allow the flavors to meld together.

5. Sprinkle sesame seeds over the salad before serving.

13.2 Grilled Eggplant with Miso Glaze:
Ingredients:

- 2 medium eggplants, sliced into rounds
- 2 tablespoons miso paste
- 2 tablespoons mirin
- 1 tablespoon soy sauce
- 1 tablespoon honey or maple syrup
- Vegetable oil, for grilling

Instructions:

1. Preheat your grill to medium-high heat.
2. In a small bowl, whisk together the miso paste, mirin, soy sauce, and honey (or maple syrup) to create the glaze.
3. Brush both sides of the eggplant slices with vegetable oil to prevent sticking.
4. Grill the eggplant slices for about 2-3 minutes per side, or until grill marks appear.
5. Brush the miso glaze onto one side of the eggplant slices and continue grilling for another 1-2 minutes.
6. Flip the slices, brush the other side with the glaze, and grill for an additional 1-2 minutes.
7. Remove from the grill and serve the grilled eggplant slices hot.

13.3 Japanese Potato Salad:
Ingredients:

- 4 large potatoes, peeled and cubed
- 1 carrot, peeled and diced
- 1/2 cup frozen peas, thawed
- 1/4 cup mayonnaise
- 1 tablespoon rice vinegar
- 1 teaspoon sugar
- Salt and pepper, to taste

Instructions:

1. Place the cubed potatoes and diced carrot in a pot of salted water. Bring to a boil and cook until the potatoes are fork-tender.
2. Drain the potatoes and carrots, then transfer them to a large mixing bowl.
3. Add the thawed peas, mayonnaise, rice vinegar, sugar, salt, and pepper to the bowl.
4. Gently mix all the ingredients together until well combined.
5. Taste and adjust the seasoning if needed.
6. Chill the potato salad in the refrigerator for at least 1 hour before serving.

13.4 Sesame Soy Edamame:
Ingredients:

- 1 pound edamame, in the pod
- 2 tablespoons soy sauce
- 1 tablespoon sesame oil
- 1 tablespoon sesame seeds
- Chili flakes (optional), for added heat

Instructions:

1. Steam or boil the edamame pods according to package instructions until they are tender.
2. Drain the edamame and transfer them to a bowl.
3. In a separate small bowl, whisk together the soy sauce, sesame oil, sesame seeds, and chili flakes (if desired).
4. Pour the sauce over the edamame and toss to coat evenly.
5. Serve the sesame soy edamame as a flavorful and addictive side dish.

13.5 Mixed Green Salad with Ponzu Dressing:
Ingredients:

- 4 cups mixed salad greens
- 1/2 cucumber, thinly sliced
- 1/2 carrot, julienned
- 1/4 cup radishes, thinly sliced
- 2 tablespoons ponzu sauce
- 1 tablespoon sesame oil
- Sesame seeds, for garnish

Instructions:

1. In a large salad bowl, combine the mixed salad greens, sliced cucumber, julienned carrot, and sliced radishes.
2. In a separate small bowl, whisk together the ponzu sauce and sesame oil to create the dressing.
3. Drizzle the dressing over the salad and toss gently to coat.
4. Sprinkle sesame seeds over the salad for added crunch and flavor.
5. Serve the mixed green salad with ponzu dressing alongside the yakitori skewers.

These side dishes and salads provide a refreshing contrast to the smoky and savory flavors of yakitori. Experiment with different combinations and add your own creative twists to customize the meal according to your preferences. With a balance of vibrant vegetables, tangy dressings, and complementary flavors, you'll create a well-rounded yakitori dining experience.

Chapter 14: Yakitori for Every Season: Seasonal Ingredients and Grilling Tips

Yakitori is a versatile dish that can be enjoyed throughout the year by incorporating seasonal ingredients. In this chapter, we will explore the beauty of yakitori for every season, highlighting the best ingredients to use during different times of the year. Additionally, we'll provide grilling tips specific to each season, ensuring your yakitori is perfectly cooked and bursting with flavors that celebrate the season.

14.1 Spring Yakitori:

Spring brings an abundance of fresh and vibrant ingredients. Here are some suggestions for spring-inspired yakitori:

Cherry Blossom Chicken Skewers: Marinate chicken pieces in a mixture of soy sauce, mirin, sake, sugar, and a touch of cherry blossom syrup for a delicate floral flavor. Grill the skewers until tender and fragrant.

Asparagus and Bacon Wraps: Take advantage of the tender asparagus spears that are in season. Wrap each spear with a strip of bacon and grill until the bacon is crispy and the asparagus is cooked through.

Grilling Tips for Spring:

Embrace the freshness: Spring ingredients shine with their natural flavors, so keep the seasoning simple to let the ingredients speak for themselves.

Moderate heat: Use medium heat on the grill to ensure even cooking without scorching the delicate spring ingredients.

14.2 Summer Yakitori:

Summer brings an array of vibrant colors and bold flavors. Here are some summer-inspired yakitori ideas:

Watermelon and Feta Skewers: Alternate cubes of juicy watermelon and salty feta cheese on skewers. Grill briefly to lightly char the watermelon and enhance its sweetness.

Grilled Corn with Miso Butter: Grill whole corn cobs until they are slightly charred. Brush them with a mixture of miso paste and butter for a savory and rich glaze.

Grilling Tips for Summer:

High heat for char: Summer is the perfect time to embrace the smoky and charred flavors. Use high heat to achieve a nice char on the ingredients without overcooking them.

Quick and frequent basting: Summer ingredients often benefit from quick basting with flavorful marinades or sauces to keep them moist and add an extra layer of taste.

14.3 Autumn Yakitori:

Autumn brings a harvest of rich and earthy flavors. Here are some autumn-inspired yakitori suggestions:

Mushroom Medley Skewers: Thread a variety of autumn mushrooms, such as shiitake, cremini, and oyster mushrooms, onto skewers. Grill until tender and aromatic.

Maple-Glazed Sweet Potato Skewers: Cut sweet potatoes into cubes, brush them with a mixture of maple syrup, soy sauce, and a pinch of cinnamon, and grill until caramelized and tender.

Grilling Tips for Autumn:

Medium-low heat: Autumn ingredients often benefit from gentle and slow cooking to bring out their natural sweetness. Use medium-low heat to achieve a tender and flavorful result.

Warm spices: Embrace the flavors of autumn by incorporating warm spices like cinnamon, nutmeg, and cloves into your marinades or sauces.

14.4 Winter Yakitori:

Winter is a time for hearty and comforting flavors. Here are some winter-inspired yakitori ideas:

Teriyaki Glazed Beef Skewers: Marinate beef cubes in a homemade teriyaki sauce with soy sauce, mirin, sake, sugar, and garlic. Grill until the beef is cooked to your desired doneness and the glaze is caramelized.

Bacon-Wrapped Quail Eggs: Wrap quail eggs with bacon and secure with a toothpick. Grill until the bacon is crispy and the eggs are heated through.

Grilling Tips for Winter:

Preheat the grill: Winter weather may require a longer preheating time for your grill. Make sure to preheat it thoroughly to maintain a consistent cooking temperature.

Keep it warm: Consider serving your yakitori on a preheated platter or keeping them in a covered dish to retain their warmth in colder temperatures.

By embracing seasonal ingredients and following these grilling tips, you can make the most of each season and create yakitori dishes that truly celebrate the flavors of the time. Adapt your recipes to incorporate the best ingredients available during each season, and experiment with different combinations to find your favorite seasonal yakitori creations.

Chapter 15: Yakitori-Inspired Bites: Creative Recipes Beyond Skewers

While yakitori skewers are the traditional form of this delicious grilled dish, the flavors and techniques can be applied to create a variety of yakitori-inspired bites. In this chapter, we will explore creative recipes that go beyond skewers, incorporating the essence of yakitori into new and exciting culinary creations. From sliders to rice bowls and savory pancakes, these recipes will expand your yakitori repertoire and introduce unique flavors and textures to your dining experience.

15.1 Yakitori Sliders:
   Ingredients:

- 1 pound ground chicken or beef
- 2 tablespoons soy sauce
- 2 tablespoons mirin
- 1 tablespoon sake
- 1 tablespoon sugar
- Slider buns
- Lettuce, tomato slices, and other desired toppings

Instructions:

1. In a bowl, combine the ground chicken or beef with soy sauce, mirin, sake, and sugar. Mix well to incorporate the flavors.
2. Divide the meat mixture into small patties, sized to fit the slider buns.
3. Preheat a grill or stovetop grill pan over medium-high heat.
4. Grill the patties for about 4-5 minutes per side, or until cooked through.
5. Toast the slider buns on the grill for a minute or until lightly browned.
6. Assemble the sliders by placing a grilled patty on each bun, topping with lettuce, tomato slices, and any other desired toppings.
7. Serve the yakitori sliders hot.

15.2 Yakitori Rice Bowl:
Ingredients:

- Cooked rice
- Yakitori skewers (choose your preferred protein, such as chicken, beef, or tofu)
- Yakitori sauce (refer to Chapter 3 for classic yakitori sauce recipe)
- Steamed vegetables (such as broccoli, carrots, or snap peas)
- Pickled ginger, for garnish
- Chopped green onions, for garnish
- Sesame seeds, for garnish

Instructions:

1. Prepare a bowl of cooked rice as the base.
2. Grill the yakitori skewers according to the specific recipe in Chapter 5 or Chapter 6.
3. Remove the cooked yakitori from the skewers and slice them into bite-sized pieces.
4. Place the yakitori pieces on top of the rice.
5. Drizzle yakitori sauce over the rice and yakitori.
6. Add steamed vegetables on the side.
7. Garnish with pickled ginger, chopped green onions, and sesame seeds.
8. Mix everything together before enjoying the yakitori rice bowl.

15.3 Yakitori Okonomiyaki (Japanese Savory Pancake):
Ingredients:

- 1 cup all-purpose flour
- 1/2 cup dashi (Japanese soup stock)
- 2 eggs
- 1 cup shredded cabbage
- 1/4 cup chopped green onions
- Yakitori skewers (choose your preferred protein, such as chicken, pork, or shrimp)
- Yakitori sauce (refer to Chapter 3 for classic yakitori sauce recipe)
- Mayonnaise
- Bonito flakes (optional)
- Pickled ginger (optional)

Instructions:

1. In a large bowl, combine the all-purpose flour, dashi, and eggs. Whisk until smooth.
2. Add the shredded cabbage and chopped green onions to the batter. Mix well to incorporate.
3. Preheat a non-stick skillet or griddle over medium heat and lightly oil the surface.
4. Pour a ladleful of the batter onto the skillet to form a round pancake shape.
5. Place a few pieces of grilled yakitori on top of the pancake while it's cooking.
6. Cook the pancake for about 3-4 minutes on each side, or until golden brown and cooked through.
7. Drizzle yakitori sauce and mayonnaise over the cooked pancake.
8. Optional: Sprinkle bonito flakes and add pickled ginger for extra flavor and garnish.

9. Slice the pancake into wedges and serve it hot.

These yakitori-inspired bites offer a fresh and unique twist on the traditional skewers, allowing you to explore new flavors and presentation styles. Whether you're craving sliders, a satisfying rice bowl, or a savory pancake, these recipes will bring the essence of yakitori to your table in exciting and delicious ways.

Chapter 16: Yakitori Desserts: Sweet Endings from the Grill

Yakitori isn't just limited to savory delights. The grill can also be used to create delectable desserts and sweet treats with a yakitori twist. In this chapter, we will explore the world of yakitori-inspired desserts, where smoky flavors and caramelization combine with sweet ingredients to create irresistible dishes. From grilled fruit skewers to caramelized treats, these dessert recipes will provide the perfect sweet ending to your yakitori feast.

16.1 Grilled Pineapple Skewers with Cinnamon Sugar:
Ingredients:

- Fresh pineapple, cut into chunks
- 2 tablespoons melted butter
- 2 tablespoons brown sugar
- 1 teaspoon ground cinnamon

Instructions:

1. Preheat the grill to medium-high heat.
2. Thread the pineapple chunks onto skewers.
3. In a small bowl, combine the melted butter, brown sugar, and ground cinnamon.
4. Brush the pineapple skewers with the cinnamon sugar mixture, coating them evenly.
5. Grill the skewers for about 3-4 minutes per side, or until the pineapple is lightly charred and caramelized.
6. Remove from the grill and serve the grilled pineapple skewers hot.

16.2 Yakitori-Inspired S'mores:
Ingredients:

- Graham crackers
- Marshmallows
- Chocolate bars
- Yakitori skewers

Instructions:

1. Preheat the grill to medium heat.
2. Assemble the s'mores by placing a piece of chocolate on half of the graham crackers.
3. Skewer the marshmallows onto the yakitori skewers.
4. Grill the marshmallows over indirect heat, turning them occasionally, until they are golden brown and slightly melted.
5. Remove the skewered marshmallows from the grill and carefully slide them onto the chocolate-covered graham crackers.
6. Top with the remaining graham crackers to create the s'mores sandwiches.
7. Allow the heat from the marshmallows to slightly melt the chocolate before enjoying the yakitori-inspired s'mores.

16.3 Grilled Banana Split:
Ingredients:

- Ripe bananas, unpeeled
- Vanilla ice cream
- Chocolate sauce
- Whipped cream
- Chopped nuts (such as peanuts or almonds)
- Maraschino cherries

Instructions:

1. Preheat the grill to medium-high heat.
2. Leave the bananas unpeeled and place them on the grill grates.
3. Grill the bananas for about 4-5 minutes per side, or until the peels turn black and the bananas inside become soft and caramelized.
4. Remove the bananas from the grill and let them cool slightly.
5. Carefully peel the bananas and slice them lengthwise.
6. Arrange the grilled banana slices in a serving dish.
7. Top the grilled bananas with scoops of vanilla ice cream.
8. Drizzle chocolate sauce over the ice cream and bananas.
9. Garnish with whipped cream, chopped nuts, and maraschino cherries.
10. Serve the grilled banana split immediately.

16.4 Honey-Glazed Grilled Peaches:
Ingredients:

- Ripe peaches, halved and pitted
- Honey
- Fresh mint leaves, for garnish

Instructions:

1. Preheat the grill to medium-high heat.
2. Brush the cut sides of the peach halves with honey, coating them generously.
3. Place the peach halves on the grill, cut side down.
4. Grill the peaches for about 3-4 minutes per side, or until they are tender and grill marks appear.
5. Remove the grilled peaches from the heat and transfer them to a serving plate.
6. Drizzle more honey over the peaches, if desired.
7. Garnish with fresh mint leaves.
8. Serve the honey-glazed grilled peaches warm.

These yakitori-inspired desserts offer a delightful blend of smoky flavors, caramelization, and sweetness. From grilled pineapple skewers to yakitori s'mores, these treats will satisfy your sweet tooth and provide a unique ending to your yakitori feast.

With the inclusion of these creative and mouthwatering dessert recipes, you can now create a complete yakitori dining experience from start to finish. Enjoy exploring the world of yakitori-inspired dishes and delight in the flavors that this traditional Japanese grilling technique brings to your table.

Chapter 17: Yakitori for Kids: Family-Friendly Recipes and Tips

Yakitori is a versatile and delicious dish that can be enjoyed by the whole family, including kids. In this chapter, we will explore family-friendly yakitori recipes and provide tips for making the dining experience enjoyable and engaging for children. From simple flavors to fun presentation ideas, these recipes and tips will help you introduce yakitori to your kids and create memorable family meals together.

17.1 Teriyaki Chicken Skewers:

Ingredients:

- Boneless, skinless chicken thighs, cut into bite-sized pieces
- 2 tablespoons soy sauce
- 2 tablespoons mirin
- 1 tablespoon sake
- 1 tablespoon sugar
- Bamboo skewers, soaked in water

Instructions:

1. In a bowl, combine soy sauce, mirin, sake, and sugar to make the teriyaki sauce.
2. Thread the chicken pieces onto the soaked bamboo skewers.
3. Preheat a grill or stovetop grill pan over medium-high heat.
4. Grill the chicken skewers for about 4-5 minutes per side, or until cooked through.
5. During the last minute of grilling, brush the teriyaki sauce onto the skewers.
6. Remove from the grill and let the skewers cool slightly before

serving.

17.2 Vegetable Yakitori Skewers:
Ingredients:

- Assorted kid-friendly vegetables, such as cherry tomatoes, bell peppers, zucchini, and mushrooms
- Olive oil
- Salt and pepper
- Bamboo skewers, soaked in water

Instructions:

1. Preheat a grill or stovetop grill pan over medium-high heat.
2. Cut the vegetables into bite-sized pieces, ensuring they are large enough for easy skewering.
3. Toss the vegetables with olive oil, salt, and pepper to lightly coat.
4. Thread the vegetables onto the soaked bamboo skewers, alternating between different types.
5. Grill the vegetable skewers for about 3-4 minutes per side, or until the vegetables are tender and lightly charred.
6. Remove from the grill and let the skewers cool slightly before serving.

17.3 Yakitori Rice Balls:
Ingredients:

- Cooked Japanese short-grain rice
- Nori seaweed sheets, cut into thin strips
- Kid-friendly fillings, such as teriyaki chicken, grilled vegetables, or scrambled eggs

- Salt, for seasoning (optional)

Instructions:

1. Take a small handful of cooked rice and shape it into a ball using wet hands.
2. Create an indentation in the rice ball and fill it with the desired kid-friendly filling.
3. Close the rice ball and shape it back into a smooth ball.
4. Wrap a strip of nori seaweed around the rice ball, securing it in place.
5. Repeat the process with the remaining rice and fillings.
6. Season the rice balls with a sprinkle of salt, if desired.
7. Serve the yakitori rice balls at room temperature or slightly chilled.

Tips for Kid-Friendly Yakitori Dining:

Engage kids in the cooking process: Involve children in the preparation and assembly of the yakitori skewers or rice balls. Let them assist with threading the ingredients onto the skewers or shaping the rice balls. This not only helps develop their culinary skills but also increases their interest and excitement in the meal.

Serve with dipping sauces: Offer a variety of kid-friendly dipping sauces, such as a mild soy sauce or teriyaki sauce, alongside the yakitori. Kids enjoy interactive dining experiences, and dipping the skewers or rice balls into flavorful sauces can make the meal more enjoyable for them.

Make it fun: Consider creating themed yakitori meals for kids. For example, you can arrange the skewers to resemble animals or create character-shaped rice balls. Playful presentations and a touch of creativity can make the dining experience more appealing to children.

Offer a balance: Accompany the yakitori with kid-friendly side dishes, such as steamed rice, sliced fruits, or simple salads. This ensures a well-rounded meal and provides options for kids who may be hesitant to try new flavors.

Be mindful of spice levels: When seasoning or marinating the yakitori, consider reducing the amount of spice or heat to suit kids' palates. Opt for milder flavors that are more familiar to children.

By incorporating these family-friendly recipes and tips, you can introduce your kids to the flavors of yakitori and create enjoyable dining experiences that the whole family can cherish. Experiment with different ingredients, engage your children in the cooking process, and make the meal fun and interactive. With these strategies, yakitori can become a family favorite that brings joy and togetherness to your table.

Chapter 18: Health Benefits of Yakitori: Lean Proteins and Grilled Goodness

Yakitori not only offers a delicious and flavorful dining experience but also provides several health benefits. In this chapter, we will explore the nutritional advantages of yakitori, focusing on its lean protein content and the grilling method that enhances the flavors while minimizing the need for added fats. Understanding the health benefits of yakitori can help you make informed choices about incorporating this delectable dish into your balanced and nutritious diet.

18.1 Lean Protein Source:

Yakitori primarily consists of skewered and grilled protein, typically chicken, but it can also include other lean meats, seafood, and plant-based alternatives. Here are some key health benefits of yakitori as a lean protein source:

Muscle Development and Repair: Protein is essential for building and repairing muscles. Yakitori provides a concentrated source of high-quality protein, promoting muscle development and recovery after physical activity.

Satiety and Weight Management: Protein-rich foods like yakitori help increase feelings of fullness and satiety, which can aid in weight management by reducing overeating and snacking between meals.

Nutrient Density: Lean proteins found in yakitori contain essential nutrients such as vitamins (e.g., vitamin B12, niacin) and minerals (e.g., iron, zinc), contributing to overall health and well-being.

Lower Calorie Content: Compared to fatty cuts of meat or processed alternatives, yakitori made with lean proteins tends to have a lower calorie content, making it a healthier choice for those watching their calorie intake.

18.2 Grilled Goodness:

The grilling method used in yakitori preparation offers additional health benefits:

Reduced Fat Content: Grilling yakitori allows excess fat to drip off the skewers, resulting in lower fat content compared to other cooking methods like deep-frying or pan-frying. This makes yakitori a healthier option for those aiming to reduce their fat intake.

Retained Nutrients: Grilling quickly seals in the natural flavors and nutrients of the ingredients, preserving their nutritional value. This ensures that you can enjoy the benefits of vitamins, minerals, and antioxidants present in the lean proteins and vegetables used in yakitori.

Minimal Need for Added Fats: The flavors in yakitori come from the ingredients themselves, reducing the reliance on added fats and sauces for taste. This can be beneficial for those seeking to reduce their intake of unhealthy fats and excess sodium.

Smoky Flavors without Heavy Seasonings: Grilling imparts a smoky and charred flavor to the yakitori without the need for heavy seasonings or excessive salt. This makes yakitori a healthier alternative to dishes that rely on heavy sauces or flavorings.

It is important to note that the overall healthiness of yakitori depends on the choices you make regarding the ingredients and cooking techniques. Opting for lean cuts of meat, fresh seafood, and well-balanced plant-based alternatives ensures that you derive the maximum health benefits from your yakitori dishes.

As with any food, moderation and variety are key. Incorporating a diverse range of vegetables, whole grains, and other nutritious foods alongside yakitori can contribute to a well-rounded and wholesome diet.

In this cookbook, we have delved into the world of yakitori, a beloved Japanese dish of grilled skewers. From the rich history and tradition of yakitori to exploring its various flavors, techniques, and regional variations, we have covered a wide range of topics to help you become a yakitori master in your own kitchen.

Starting with the introduction to yakitori and its cultural significance, we then delved into essential tools and ingredients needed for yakitori preparation. We provided detailed recipes for classic chicken yakitori, as well as explored variations with pork, beef, seafood, and even vegetarian options. We also ventured into the realm of vegetable yakitori, showcasing the versatility of grilling greens.

The cookbook covered chapters on yakitori sauce variations, mastering grilling techniques, dips and accompaniments, yakitori for special diets, and the pros and cons of grilling with charcoal versus gas. We also provided recipes and tips for yakitori sides, explored seasonal ingredients and grilling tips, and even ventured into the world of yakitori-inspired bites, desserts, and sweet treats.

We covered the importance of making yakitori a family-friendly dish with recipes and tips specifically designed for kids. We discussed the health benefits of yakitori as a lean protein source and highlighted the advantages of the grilling method. We even explored the art of garnishing and plating yakitori to create visually appealing presentations that enhance the dining experience.

Lastly, we took a culinary journey through the different prefectures of Japan, exploring regional yakitori flavors and highlighting unique ingredients, marinades, and grilling techniques.

With this comprehensive cookbook, you are equipped with the knowledge and recipes to create delicious yakitori dishes right in your own kitchen. Whether you're a seasoned chef or a beginner, these recipes and insights will guide you on a flavorful and satisfying yakitori adventure.

So, fire up your grill, gather your favorite ingredients, and let the aroma of sizzling skewers fill the air. Embrace the art of yakitori and enjoy the experience of sharing these delectable grilled delights with family and friends. May your culinary journey be filled with joy, exploration, and the irresistible flavors of yakitori. Happy grilling!